SCOTLAND
A PICTURE BOOK TO REMEMBER HER BY

© *Illustrations:* Colour Library International Ltd. 1977

First published in Great Britain in 1975 by
Colour Library International Limited, England.

Designed and Produced by Ted Smart C.L.I.

Printed and bound by L.E.G.O. Vicenza Italy

Filmsetting by Focus Photoset 90-94 Clerkenwell Road, London EC1, England

ISBN 0 904681 36 x

Published by Crescent Books, a division of
Crown Publishers Inc.
All rights reserved.
CRESCENT 1978

CRESCENT BOOKS

Loch Lubnaig, Perthshire *(Below)*
The road from the lovely village of Strathyre to Callander winds along the eastern shore of Loch Lubnaig. Each turn of the road presents new and memorable views of the loch in its lovely wooded setting.

Loch Insh, Inverness-shire *(Top Left)*
Lovely Loch Insh is an enlargement of the fast-flowing river Spey, a river noted for its excellent salmon fishing. The loch itself is often referred to as "the home and hold of the big pike".

Loch Affric, Inverness-shire *(Below Left)*
Like a jewel on a cloak of mountain and moorland, Loch Affric lies in one of the loveliest glens in Scotland. The district is noted for its richly-wooded scenery, particularly the pines and birches and it was in such country that the fugitive Bonnie Prince Charlie hid after the defeat of his cause at Culloden.

Glen Etive, Argyllshire *(Above)*
The bulk of the Great Shepherd of Etive dominates this view of one of Scotland's most impressive glens. The river Etive flows through the glen carrying waters that have risen in the far off Black Corries of Rannoch Moor.

Wick Harbour, Caithness *(Top Left)*
The Norse word Vik–'a bay'–gives the name to and the location of this ancient Royal burgh and important northern fishing station. Situated at the mouth of the Wick water where it enters the bay, the harbour bears the stamp of two of Scotland's famous engineers… Telford, who designed it and Stevenson who later improved it.

Ayr Harbour Ayrshire *(Below)*
Much changed since the days of the poet, Ayr is a natural choice of starting point for touring the Burns Country. From the harbour the seaward view is impressive and beyond the bulk of Ailsa Craig it is possible to discern the Irish coastline.

The Harbour, Aberdeen *(Below Left)*
Although still a fishing port and the home of deep sea trawlers, Aberdeen harbour is now a busy base for vessels concerned with North Sea oil operations. The city is affectionately known as "The Granite City" from the extensive use of that particular stone in many of its buildings.

Crail, Fifeshire *(Above)*
Crail is an attractive ancient Royal Burgh on the "East Neuk" of Fife.
The small harbour is flanked by picturesque red-tiled houses with
crow-stepped gables that are a constant delight to the many artists
who try to capture their unique charm.

Tobermory, Isle of Mull *(Below)*
Over the years many have searched for a sign of the treasure that is
thought to lie in the wreck of the Spanish Armada galleon *Florencia*
…blown up and sunk in the bay in 1588. But on the surface there is
no need to search, for the treasure of Tobermory is to be found in the
natural charm of the town itself and its attractively wooded setting.

Largs, Ayrshire *(Top Right)*
Largs was the scene of a decisive battle between the forces of Alexander III and the King of Norway in 1263 but today it is a happy holiday resort with a bracing climate. The town looks across the Clyde to Cowal, Bute and the unmistakable Isle of Arran.

Rothesay, Isle of Bute *(Below)*
On a sandy bay overlooking the Firth of Clyde, Rothesay is a popular resort "doon the watter" from Glasgow. Near the pier is the site of the old castle, largely destroyed in the 17th century, while the original castle is said to have been destroyed by Robert the Bruce.

Findochty, Banffshire *(Bottom Right)*
Situated on a rocky part of the coast on the eastern side of Spey Bay is the village of Findochty. The harbour is a natural attraction to visitors of all ages and is one of many such havens dotted along this coastline.

The Crinan Canal, Argyllshire *(Below)*
Connecting Loch Fyne and the Firth of Clyde with the Western Isles, the Crinan Canal is situated in an area of great natural beauty. Construction of the canal began in 1793 and although it was opened in 1801 it was not fully completed until 1817.

The Cuillins, Isle of Skye *(Top Right)*
The romantic Isle of Skye is the setting for the magnificent Cuillins... a mountain range of serrated peaks and wild corries. The grandeur of the main ridges, the Black Cuillins, extends in a semi-circle some six miles in length.

Glen Clova and the Grampians, Angus *(Bottom Right)*
One of the lovely glens of Angus, Clova leads into the heart of Grampian mountains. This area is extremely popular with hill wa' although the views from the road circling the glen are rewarding.

Abbotsford, Roxburghshire *(Top Left)*
This well-known home of Sir Walter Scott is in a pleasantly secluded setting close to the river Tweed. Here it is possible to see the chair and desk where he worked as well as many of the interesting items that the author collected over the years.

Fettes College, Edinburgh *(Above)*
One of the great British public schools Fettes is set in spacious grounds, much of which are devoted to sporting activities. Founded by a former twice Lord Provost of Edinburgh, Sir William Fettes, Bart. the school admitted its first pupil in October 1870.

Elgin Cathedral, Morayshire *(Bottom Left)*
Although in ruins the magnificence of Elgin Cathedral as it once was is still apparent. Founded in 1224 by Bishop Andrew of Moray the cathedral was considered "inferior to few in Europe" and it was often referred to as the "Lantern of the North".

Edinburgh *(Top Left)*
Viewed from the castle walls are two of the capital's best-known buildings, the Royal Scottish Academy and beside it, the National Gallery of Scotland—considered to be one of the more important of the smaller European galleries. Rising from the Princes Street Gardens is the familiar shape of the Scott Monument.

Argyle Street, Glasgow *(Below)*
Argyle Street is a shopper's paradise in the heart of ever-growing Glasgow. A particular feature of the street familiar to all Glaswegians is the "Highlandman's umbrella"...where the railway to Central Station crosses the busy thoroughfare thus providing an inexpensive umbrella for the canniest of Scots!

St. Andrews, Fifeshire *(Below Left)*
St. Andrews was once the ecclesiastical capital of Scotland and was the site of the largest cathedral in the country. Although now in ruins, portions of the twelfth century walls still exist and the ground plan can still be traced.

Abbotsford House, Roxburghshire *(Above)*

Dating from 1817, Abbotsford House, the last home of Sir Walter Scott who died here in 1832, stands on the banks of the lovely River Tweed. Surrounded by magnificent woods, Abbotsford holds many relics of the author, and the study in particular, has been preserved as he left it. To the south-east rise the beautiful Eildon Hills, affording wonderful views of the Scott Country.

Culzean Castle, Ayrshire *(Top Left)*

A splendid edifice, the castle dates from 1777 and holds a commanding position overlooking the sweep of Culzean Bay. A stronghold of the Kennedys for many years, the building contains many interesting relics of the family. A flat in the castle was presented to General Eisenhower as a Scottish residence during his lifetime. The grounds are of particular beauty and are open to visitors during the summer months.

Blair Castle, Blair Atholl, Perthshire *(Bottom Left)*

Set in its own wooded grounds, Blair Castle is the seat of the Duke of Atholl and is open to the public. It is unique in being the headquarters of the only private army in the realm – the Duke's own bodyguard received its colours from Queen Victoria in 1845. The nearby village of Blair Atholl is an excellent centre for exploring the many glens that meet here.

Inverary Castle, Argyllshire *(Right)*

One of the best known castles in Scotland, Inverary – for long the hereditary seat of the Dukes of Argyll – is situated on the bank of the river Aray. The present castle dates from 1745 and is seen at its best in sunshine immediately after a shower of rain when it appears to change colour.

Dunure Castle, Ayrshire *(Below)*
This beautiful sunset at Dunure shows the fragmentary remains of the castle on the cliffs in silhouette and gives no hint of a cruel Earl of Cassillis who is said to have roasted Allan Stewart, commendator of Crossraguel Abbey, over a slow fire until the victim consented to surrender the abbey lands. Dunure is a popular seaside resort and fishing village.

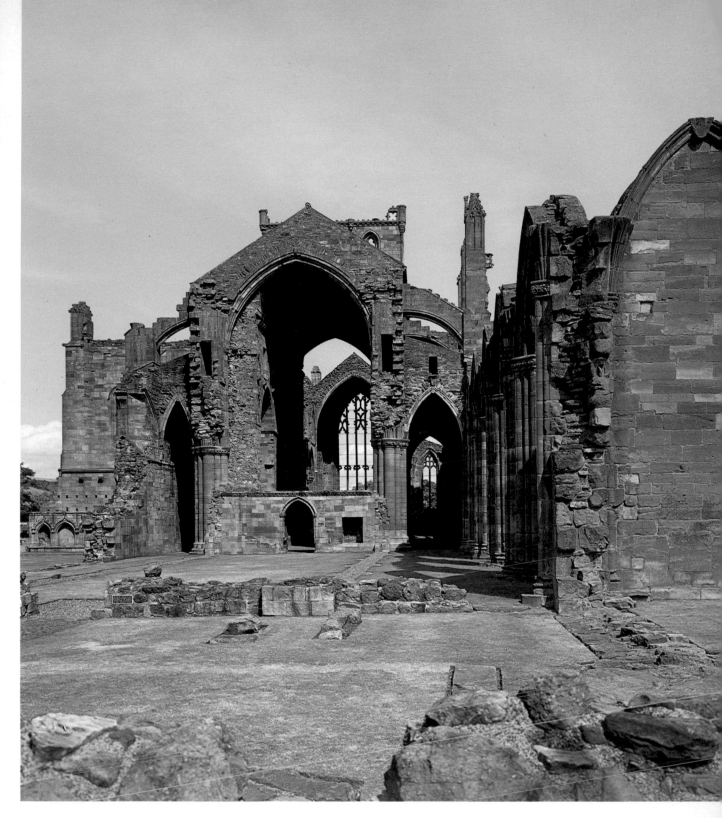

Melrose Abbey, Roxburghshire *(Above)*
Beautiful Melrose Abbey is one of the prime attractions of the
border county of Roxburgh. Founded in 1136 by David I, the
abbey suffered from many later invasions and was used as a
quarry after the Reformation. Gifted to the nation in 1918 by
the Duke of Buccleuch, it has many associations with Scottish
Royalty and the heart of Robert the Bruce is buried beneath the
High Altar.

George Square, Glasgow, Lanarkshire *(Below)*
The elaborate granite building of the City Chambers looks out onto George Square, the Cenotaph designed by Sir John Burnet and the 80 ft. high monument bearing a statue of Sir Walter Scott. The attractive gardens, ablaze with flowers, are a haven for the people of this busy city.

Sunset on the Clyde, Glasgow *(Top Right)*
The magnificent River Clyde with its immense docks and extensive shipbuilding industry is world famous. The city of Glasgow has grown and expanded over the past 150 years, and is Scotland's largest city and seaport. Silhouetted against the sunset, the cranes and masts of Clydeside reach up to the sky while the smooth glittering river flows gently down past Greenock and Dunoon, to the Firth of Clyde and the Atlantic Ocean.

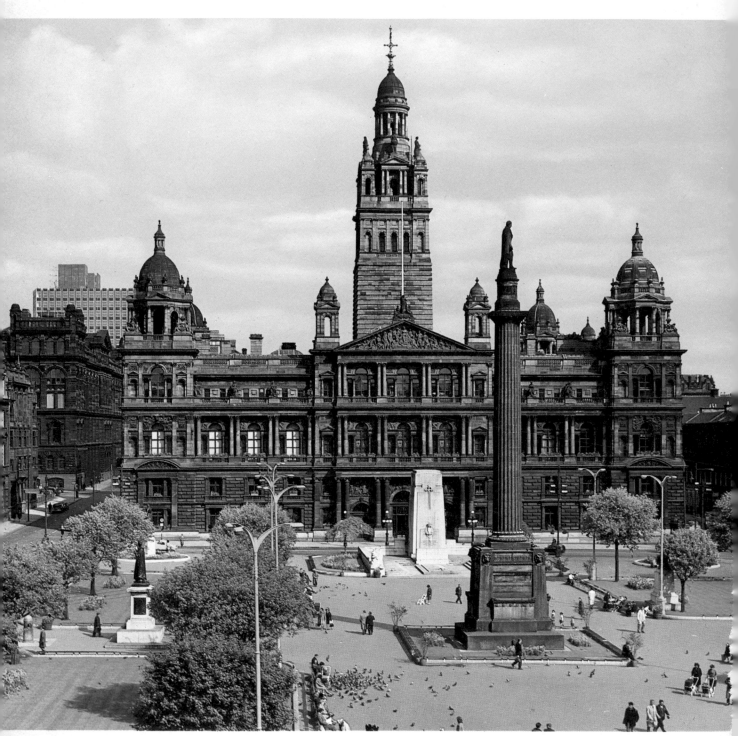

University and Art Gallery, Glasgow *(Bottom Right)*
Glasgow University, founded in 1450, is particularly noted for its library containing many rare books. Nearby the Museum and Art Gallery, opened in 1901, house the famous Burrell Collection, together with one of the most comprehensive collections of paintings in Britain, representing Scottish, Dutch and French artists.

Firth of Clyde from Lyle Hill,
Greenock, Renfrewshire *(Below)*
Lyle Hill, Greenock, affords a magnificent view of the Firth of
Clyde, always busy with shipping. The famous Cross of
Lorraine was erected on Lyle Hill, in memory of the Free French
sailors who gave their lives in the Battle of the Atlantic during
the second World War.

Queen Elizabeth II Passing Cloch Point,
Renfrewshire *(Top Right)*
Cloch Point overlooks the Clyde Estuary opposite the popular
resort and yachting centre of Dunoon. The famous Cloch Point
Lighthouse, built in 1797, is a well-known landmark. The grace-
ful liner, Queen Elizabeth II, built on Clydeside, was launched in
September, 1967.

Cardwell Bay and Gourock, Renfrewshire *(Bottom Right)*
Gourock lies on a sheltered bay on the Firth of Clyde and is a
popular holiday and yachting resort. Across the Firth lie Holy
Loch and Loch Long, with their magnificent surrounding
scenery. On the summit of Lyle Hill, from which this view is
taken, stands the Cross of Lorraine, erected in memory of
those Free French who died in the Battle of the Atlantic.

Ross Fountain and The Castle, Edinburgh *(Below)*

The origins of Edinburgh Castle are lost in history. An impressive fortress, it overlooks Princes Street and the attractive Old Town. It has changed hands many times in the course of the years and is the scene of many historic events. The famous Prince Charles Edward — 'Bonnie Prince Charlie' — although holding the town, did not succeed in capturing the Castle. In the foreground, stands the ornate Ross Fountain, built in Paris for the Paris Exhibition by Daniel Ross, a gun maker, and gifted by him to Edinburgh in 1869.

Princes Street, Edinburgh *(Top Right)*

The busy thoroughfare of Princes Street runs through the heart of this historic city, the capital of Scotland. Dominating the scene is the famous castle, its origins lost in legendary time. From the castle, the High Street or Royal Mile leads to the Palace of Holyroodhouse and Holyrood Park which includes Arthur's Seat, a rugged extinct volcano commanding fine views of the city and its extensive docks on the Firth of Forth.

Edinburgh by Night, Midlothian *(Bottom Right)*

The National Monument and Nelson Monument stand on Calton Hill from whence we look down over the lighted streets of the town. In the background is the Castle, steeped in history and originally known as ''Duneadain'' or the ''fort on a hill''. To the left is the spire of the ancient Greyfriars Church, built in 1612.

Firth of Clyde from Lyle Hill,
Greenock, Renfrewshire *(Below)*
Lyle Hill, Greenock, affords a magnificent view of the Firth of Clyde, always busy with shipping. The famous Cross of Lorraine was erected on Lyle Hill, in memory of the Free French sailors who gave their lives in the Battle of the Atlantic during the second World War.

Queen Elizabeth II Passing Cloch Point,
Renfrewshire *(Top Right)*
Cloch Point overlooks the Clyde Estuary opposite the popular resort and yachting centre of Dunoon. The famous Cloch Point Lighthouse, built in 1797, is a well-known landmark. The graceful liner, Queen Elizabeth II, built on Clydeside, was launched in September, 1967.

Cardwell Bay and Gourock, Renfrewshire *(Bottom Right)*
Gourock lies on a sheltered bay on the Firth of Clyde and is a popular holiday and yachting resort. Across the Firth lie Holy Loch and Loch Long, with their magnificent surrounding scenery. On the summit of Lyle Hill, from which this view is taken, stands the Cross of Lorraine, erected in memory of those Free French who died in the Battle of the Atlantic.

The Edinburgh Military Tattoo,
Edinburgh Castle *(Left and Below)*
The Military Tattoo evolved from displays of military drill during the 1948 Edinburgh International Festival and has since become a very popular item on the programme. Although several units from overseas have taken part, the programme is mainly filled by British bands and display units. There are 27 performances during the three week Festival period, attended by many thousands of visitors from all over the world.

Forth Bridges, Midlothian *(Below)*
The setting sun reflected in the water throws these two famous bridges into relief with the graded tones of an oriental painting. Both the railway bridge, built in 1883-90, and the recent road suspension bridge beyond are staggering feats of engineering, spanning distances between 2,000 and 3,000 yards, as well as being complementary to the landscape.

The Forth Bridges from the air, Firth of Forth
(Top Right)
Two spectacular bridges span the Firth of Forth from West Lothian to Fife. The rail bridge, a magnificent feat of engineering, was built by Sir John Fowler. It is 2,765 yds. long and the two main spans are each 1,710 ft. The modern road bridge, completed in 1964, is the largest suspension bridge in Europe, being 2,000 yds. long with a centre span of 3,300 ft.

The Forth Bridges from South Queensferry, West Lothian *(Bottom Right)*

St. Andrews Golf Course, Fife *(Top and Bottom Left)*
The Royal and Ancient Golf Club of St. Andrews was founded in 1754 and today is the foremost in the world. Golf is believed to have been played here in the Fifteenth Century. Our picture shows the famous Road Hole, the Seventeenth, on the Old Course.

The Cathedral Ruins, St. Andrews, Fife *(Below)*
Built staunchly facing the cold North Sea, St. Andrews seems braced for more than just the elements. Such inflammatory matters as golf rules, John Knox's sermons and modern students' polemics are in the tradition of the town. The cathedral was founded in 1160 and is just one of the many fascinating places to visit here.

The Harbour, Crail, Fife *(Top Left)*
Crail, a very old and picturesque fishing town in the east Neuk of Fife, has many buildings dating from the Sixteenth Century. The Church, partly Thirteenth Century, is of considerable interest, as are some of the ancient carved memorials in the churchyard. Of particular charm are the old crow-stepped, and red tiled houses near the harbour.

Anstruther, Fife *(Bottom Left)*
The harbour, an important fishing port, separates Anstruther Wester from Anstruther Easter, each a Royal Burgh in its own right. Local buildings of historic interest include the Manse, a minister's house dating from 1590 and still occupied, and 16th Century unsupported Church towers which are to be found in both Burghs.

Pittenweem Harbour, Fife *(Above)*
Old houses frame the busy harbour of Pittenweem, which has been a Royal Burgh since the days of David I. This is a part of Fife once notorious for witches and as late as 1746 a woman was sentenced as a practiser of unholy arts. The imposing church tower, which resembles that of a castle, dates from 1592.

The River Tay from Kinnoull Hill, Perthshire *(Below)*
Kinnoull Hill, east of Perth, rises to a height of 729 ft. and is a
magnificent vantage point, affording fine views of the River
Tay and the 'Fair City' as well as the beautiful surrounding
countryside. From here the river flows between the fertile lands
of the Carse of Gowrie and the hills of Fife to the North Sea.

The River Tay, Perth *(Top and Bottom Right)*
Perth, 'The Fair City', stands on the River Tay, which is here
spanned by two elegant bridges. Often called 'The Gateway
to the Highlands', Perth is an important tourist centre, giving
access to much of Scotland's finest scenery. Once the capital
of Scotland, the city has many interesting historical connections.

Falls of Dochart, Killin, Perthshire *(Below)*
The picturesque River Dochart rushes down through the beautiful, deep Glen of the same name to join Loch Tay at Killin. To the north-east stately Ben Lawers, the highest mountain in Perthshire (3,984 ft.), dominates the horizon and provides good ski-ing for visitors to the popular little resort of Killin.

Falls of Orchy, Glen Orchy, Perthshire *(Top Right)*
The picturesque Falls of Orchy on the river of the same name are a well known beauty spot. Glen Orchy stretches from the Bridge of Orchy where the old and new roads to Glencoe converge, down to Dalmally in the South. Here the river flows into the long expanse of Loch Awe.

Ben Lawers and Loch Tay, Perthshire *(Bottom Right)*
Ben Lawers overlooks the large and deep Loch Tay, noted for its salmon fishing. The mountain is the highest in Perthshire and of particular botanical interest. The view from its summit, 3,984 ft., is magnificent, taking in the whole of the Breadalbane country and also the Grampians. The slopes of Ben Lawers and surrounding mountains provide good ski-ing and nearby Coire Odhar is used by the Scottish Ski Club.

The Tay Road Bridge

The new Tay road Bridge now links Dundee, Angus to Newport-on-Tay, Fife across the Firth of Tay. For many years the crossing had to be made either by rail over the famous two-mile long bridge completed in 1888 or by ferry. The previous tay Rail Bridge was blown down in a great storm in 1879.

Glamis Castle, Angus *(Right)*

Glamis Castle stands in fine grounds bordered by the Dean Water. It is one of the most notable buildings of its period in Scotland and is reputed to be ghost-haunted. The greater part of the structure dates from 1675-1687 but an older tower with 15 ft. thick walls has survived. The great sundial in the foreground is just over 21 ft. in height and has no less than 84 dials.

Dundee by Night *(Bottom Left)*

A striking panorama-by-night of the beautifully situated city and royal burgh of Dundee. Seen from Newport-on-Tay, it includes an excellent view of the Tay Road Bridge. Linking Fife with Dundee and the north, the bridge is a wonderful feat of modern engineering, completed in 1966.

Dundee and the Firth of Tay
with Fife across the River *(Below)*

Dundee, essentially a modern city with extensive docks along the Firth of Tay, has important engineering and shipbuilding industries. At Dundee the river Tay is bridged in two places. The famous rail bridge, dating from 1883, carries the main line from Edinburgh to Aberdeen and the new road bridge, completed in 1966, replaces the old car ferry to Newport-on-Tay.

Loch Tulla, Argyllshire *(Top Left)*
Bordered by the old road to Glencoe, the shores of Loch
Tulla are noted for the relics of the pines of the Caledonian
Forest. To the north, rise the bleak, undulating moors of Black
Mount and the famous peak of Stob Ghabhar, 3,565 ft. To
the south, is the attractive old Bridge of Orchy at the entrance
to Glen Orchy.

Castle Stalker, Appin, Argyllshire *(Below)*
Standing on a tiny islet in Loch Laich, off Loch Linnhe, Castle
Stalker looks on to a region familiar to readers of Robert Louis
Stevenson's Kidnapped. Following the rebellion of 1745, the
estates of the Stewarts of Appin were forfeited and put under
the management of Colin Campbell of Glenure, whose
assassination forms part of the plot of the story.

Winter in Ardgour, Argyllshire *(Bottom Left)*
The village of Ardgour is situated on the western shores of
Loch Linnhe. Garbh Bheinn, 2,903 ft., is famous among
climbers and can be reached on foot by way of the wild Coire
an Iubhair. The highest point is the 2,915 ft. high Sgurr
Dhomhail which dominates the picturesque Glen Gour.

Tarbert on Loch Fyne, Argyllshire *(Top Left)*
Sheltered in a narrow inlet off Loch Fyne, Tarbert is a happy holiday resort as well as a busy fishing port. Across the hill behind the harbour lies West Tarbert, a gateway to the islands of the Inner Hebrides.

Mull, Argyllshire *(Below)*
Part of the Inner Hebrides, the Isle of Mull guards the entrance to Loch Linnhe and is separated from the mainland by the Sound of Mull to the north and the Firth of Lorne to the south. The undulating scenery of the island is notably picturesque, particularly the rocky coastline with its many sea lochs and tiny bays and inlets. The largest town on the island is Tobermory — famed for the treasure of a Spanish galleon believed to be sunk in the Bay.

The Harbour, Oban, Argyllshire *(Bottom Left)*
Oban is finely situated on the shores of a picturesque bay landlocked by the island of Kerrera. This is a bracing summer resort, the sheltered bay giving beautiful views of sunset amid the mountains of Mull. The immense, circular stone structure known as McCaig's Folly is a vantage point for impressive views of the town and surrounding countryside.

Urquhart Castle and Loch Ness, Inverness-shire *(Top Left)*
On a rocky headland stretching out into the blue waters of
Loch Ness stands the picturesque ruin of Urquhart Castle.
Originally built in the 12th Century, this grim fortress was
sabotaged in 1692 to prevent its capture by the Jacobites.
Loch Ness of 'monster' fame is 22½ miles long and 754 ft. deep.

Aviemore, Inverness-shire *(Below)*
Nestling in the richly wooded Strath Spey which divides the
Cairngorm and Monadhliath mountains, Aviemore is a popular
Highland winter sports resort also offering fine climbing and
walking. To the east is the beautiful 12,500 acre Glen More
National Forest Park with Glenmore Lodge, a mountaineering
training centre.

The Castle, Inverness *(Bottom Left)*
Inverness Castle stands on Castle Hill affording a magnificent
view of the surrounding Highland scenery. It was built on the
site of the former stronghold, destroyed by Bonnie Prince
Charlie during the '45 rebellion. Nearby is a monument to
Flora Macdonald, the Jacobite heroine who helped the Prince
to escape after his defeat at Culloden.

Kyleakin, Isle of Sky, Inverness-shire *(Above)*
Legend has it that the princess who built Castle Moil stretched a chain across the strait — or kyle — of Akin, in order to extract a toll from ships that passed. The magic scenery of Skye, the Misty Island, tempts one to believe such tales without question.

Cuillin Hills, Skye
(Bottom Right)

Loch Laggan, Inverness-shire *(Above)*
Lying between the Monadhliath and Grampian mountains,
Loch Laggan now forms part of the Lochaber Power Scheme.
This area is beautifully wooded and offers some fine scenery,
particularly of the surrounding mountain peaks. To the north
rises Creag Meagaidh, 3,700 ft., reached by way of the wild
Coire Ardair.

**Ben Nevis from the Caledonian Canal,
Inverness-shire** *(Below)*
Winter brings an arctic hue to the Caledonian Canal which follows
the route of the Great Glen and is seen here under the shadow of
Britain's highest mountain, Ben Nevis. Opened in 1822, the
canal's total length is but 4 miles more than a straight line extend-
ing from its eastern to its western extremities.

Dunnottar Castle, Kincardineshire *(Top Left)*
The famous Dunnottar Castle stands on a rocky headland
south of Stonehaven. The tower and chapel date from the
Fourteenth Century and the gatehouse from the Sixteenth
Century. During the Commonwealth Wars, the Scottish regalia
were hidden at Dunnottar for safety, but later removed to
Kinneff Church.

The Old Bridge of Dee, near Braemar *(Below)*
The splendour of snow-clad Lochnagar makes an impressive
backcloth for the Old Bridge of Dee at Invercauld. Set in Royal
property, the old bridge dates from 1752 and from here the
river flows through Royal Deeside to the sea at Aberdeen.

The Harbour, Gourdon, Kincardineshire *(Bottom Left)*
The fishing vessels are moored and the nets are left drying in
the picturesque harbour of Gourdon. The coast line along this
part of Kincardine is extremely rocky but the harbour and
village of Gourdon are sheltered by Doolie Ness.

Union Street, Aberdeen *(Below)*
The broad, modern thoroughfare of Union Street runs through
the heart of Aberdeen. It is flanked by many famous buildings,
among them the Town House with its 200 ft. tower and the
Church of St. Nicholas. The latter was divided during the
Reformation into the East and West Churches and later rebuilt.

Aberdeen *(Top Right)*
The charters of this important city date back to 1179. Today it
represents a remarkably clean and solid picture being built
largely of granite and often referred to as 'The Granite City'. A
popular seaside resort and busy seaport, Aberdeen now plays
an increasingly important part in the servicing of the North Sea
oil rigs.

The Harbour, Aberdeen *(Bottom Right)*
This famous old city, and Royal Burgh, stands on the estuaries
of the Dee and the Don. It is often referred to as the "Granite
City", being almost entirely constructed of this stone. It is an
important port and hub of the fishing industry, besides having
a University, a Cathedral and many other buildings of historic
interest.

Macduff, Banffshire *(Below)*
Macduff, opposite the town of Banff on Banff Bay, is an important fishing town with a large harbour to accommodate the fleet of fishing vessels which put out to sea each day. Overlooking the town stands the Hill of Down, a fine viewpoint, bearing a tall war memorial.

Crovie, Banffshire *(Top Right)*
Tucked in the lee of the red cliffs of Gamrie Bay is the secluded fishing village of Crovie. Gamrie Bay has given shelter from enemies as well as the weather and St. John's church on the western arm of the bay was founded in 1004 to commemorate a Scottish victory over the marauding Danes.

Valley of the Avon, Tomintoul, Banff *(Bottom Right)*
To the east of the flat-topped Cairngorms lies the beautiful Valley of the Avon where winter sports alternate with angling to make it an all-year resort. Tomintoul, at 1,160 ft., is the highest village in the Highlands and to the north are the spectacular gorges of Glenlivet and the no-less notable whisky of the Glenlivet distillery.

Eilean Donan Castle, Ross and Cromarty *(Top Right)*
Eilean Donan Castle, the former Macrae stronghold, stands at the confluence of three lochs, Duich, Long and Alsh. Once completely surrounded by water, it is linked now by a causeway to the land. In 1719 the castle was held by a party of Spaniards in support of a Jacobite Rising and came under fire from the British frigate, 'Worcester'

Plockton, Ross and Cromarty *(Above)*
Plockton is essentially a fishing and crofting village beautifully situated on a small inlet of Loch Carron. The county of Ross and Cromarty stretches across the country from the North Sea to the Atlantic Ocean and contains every feature of scenic grandeur peculiar to the Scottish Highlands.

Loch Gairloch, Ross and Cromarty *(Bottom Right)*
Loch Gairloch lies on the west coast of Ross and Cromarty, its entrance guarded by the small island of Longa. The village of Gairloch is one of the loveliest in the Highlands, surrounded by wonderful scenery, and offering excellent bathing and fishing from its sheltered position on the eastern shore of the Loch.

Duncansby Head, Caithness *(Top Right)*
This beautiful headland, two miles east of John O' Groats, is a striking viewpoint. Just off the coast, to the south, rise the Stacks of Duncansby, three immense pillars of rock, detached from the mainland by constant sea erosion. Away to the north lie the Orkney Isles.

Badcall, Sutherland *(Above)*
The tiny, remote village of Badcall lies below Laxford Bridge where the noted salmon river, Laxford, enters Loch Laxford. A few small fishing vessels ply the island-studded Loch and the scene is dominated to the south-east by the barren, grey slopes of Ben Stack.

Dunbeath Castle, Caithness *(Bottom Right)*
Perched on the edge of the Caithness plateau, Dunbeath Castle looks deceptively prim with its 19th century facade but it preserves a 15th century keep and was worth capturing by Montrose in 1650. In the hills west of the fishing village of Dunbeath is a granite cross marking the place where tragically, the Duke of Kent's plane crashed in 1942.

Blaven, Isle of Skye *(Top Right)*
The peak of Blaven, 3,042 ft. rises to the east of the Coolins, the famous and treacherous hills of Skye. Often swathed in mist, this magnificent outcrop overlooks the beautiful Loch na Creitheach. To the east across Loch Slapin, lie the lower and less imposing Red Hills, with their rounded outlines of softer rock.

Lerwick, Shetland *(Above)*
Capital of the Shetland Islands, Lerwick is the most northerly town in Britain and a busy fishing port. Nearby, King Haco of Norway anchored while en route for the Battle of Largs in 1263. Every January, Lerwick celebrates the Norse festival of Up Helly 'A', a spectacular torchlight procession culminating in the burning of a Viking galley.

Kylesku Ferry, Sutherland *(Bottom Right)*
The vast fjord-like landscapes of the Scottish north-west coast make the scant signs of human activity seem insignificant. Among the many wild and roadless mountains, the Kylesku Ferry, looking like an insect ploughing through the water, bridges the great gap formed by the sea loch Cairnbawn and the inland lochs Glendu and Glencoul.

Crathie Church, Aberdeenshire *(Below)*
This picturesque little church dates from 1895 and the Royal Family
worship here when they are staying on Deeside. In the churchyard
is a monument erected by Queen Victoria to her faithful retainer,
John Brown.